DESCANSA EN EL PODER:
A Sacred Guide to Ancestral Communion and Artful Resistance

DENISE ZUBIZARRETA

© 2024 Denise Zubizarreta
www.TheVampDeVille.com

To my ancestors, whose whispers guide my hands and whose strength fills my spirit.

To my abuelas, who taught me the power of devotion and resilience.

And to every soul searching for the courage to reclaim their story and honor the unseen. May you find rest, power, and the truth of your lineage.

SEARCHING FOR ROOTS IN SHIFTING SANDS

My childhood felt like a collection of fragments scattered across places and people. There were pieces of New Jersey and Miami, snapshots of airports and suitcases, and the brief moments where the world seemed to pause just long enough for me to take a breath. My parents divorced when I was three, setting the rhythm for a life of constant travel between two states, two lives, and two cultures. While most kids had a single house to call home, I had a plane ticket.

Family, to me, felt like sand slipping through fingers—fleeting, intangible. My mother's father passed away when she was only a year old in Puerto Rico. His memory was a distant echo, a name in stories I never truly felt a connection to because he had left before any of us had the chance to know him. His absence was like a shadow that lingered, and I wondered what it meant to grow up without that foundational piece of my family. I often searched for glimpses of him in my mother's face, in her mannerisms, but there was only the silence of his absence.

On the other side of my family, there was my Cuban grandfather, who passed away when I was five. They say I was his best friend, and he was mine. I was told about the joy we shared, the laughter, the small rituals like him buying me orange Tic Tacs—those tiny candies that seemed to hold so much more meaning than just their sugary sweetness. I loved them then, and even now, the taste brings back an aching reminder of a connection I barely had the time to understand. His presence was warm, grounding, and brief, like a flash of sunlight before the clouds returned. His loss left a void that has never fully healed. It's an empty part of me, a space that still feels incomplete.

The duality of my childhood—moving between New Jersey and Miami—meant I was constantly learning to adapt. It wasn't just the difference in weather; it was a difference in rhythm, culture, and sense of belonging. In New Jersey, I felt the pulse of my mother's world—her stories of Puerto Rico, the essence of a past life carried in her voice and her food. In Miami, my father's Cuban roots anchored me, yet it was an anchor that drifted after my grandfather's passing. It was as though my connection to both sides of my heritage was always being pulled in different directions, never finding a true center.

Every time I touched down in a new place, it felt like I was starting over, never fully able to grow roots. School friends were temporary, homes felt more like pit stops, and the idea of belonging felt foreign. Family, which should have been the one solid ground beneath me, was fragmented by distance and loss. There was no singular sense of home—just moments and memories spread between two lives.

As I got older, I realized that my life was shaped by these absences. I was always searching, longing for the missing pieces of family that seemed to have slipped away before I could hold onto them. The legacy of my grandfathers—their stories, their presence—felt like threads of a tapestry that I was never quite able to complete. I was left to piece together a narrative with what little I knew, trying to make sense of the longing I felt for people I barely had the chance to know.

In many ways, my childhood taught me that sometimes the most meaningful connections are the ones you create in the spaces between—between flights, between homes, and between the moments when you catch a glimpse of what family could have been. It's the longing for what was lost and the hope for what remains that continue to guide me as I navigate the ever-shifting sands of my identity.

Unraveling Ancestral Threads

The journey to create this exhibition began nearly a decade ago with a simple request from my mother. She wanted to take a DNA test to uncover more about her ancestry, but she needed my help. What started as a favor turned into an unexpected, transformative journey. As I guided her through the process, something clicked within me—a curiosity, a longing to know more about how we got here, and what the true story was behind our race, identity, and culture.

The results of her DNA test sparked a fire in me that I couldn't ignore. I became obsessed with tracing our lineage, piecing together the puzzle of our family history. It was as if I was uncovering layers of hidden truths, each discovery revealing a deeper complexity than I had anticipated. On my father's side, I traced our roots back to conquistador Spaniards who had arrived in Florida early in the conquest timeline. It was a revelation that felt both distant and uncomfortably close—these were ancestors who had participated in the violent colonization of lands and people.

My mother's lineage was even more intricate. Her DNA revealed a mix of enslaved people,

Indigenous Taíno, West African, and Spanish/Portuguese ancestry. Each strand of her history held stories of survival, resilience, and resistance. The more I learned, the more I understood that our bloodline carried both the legacies of the oppressed and the oppressor. We were descendants of the colonized and the colonizers, the enslaved and the masters. It was a harsh truth, one that explained the internal battles I'd felt for as long as I could remember.

The constant feeling of being out of place, of fighting within myself, suddenly made sense. I had inherited the conflicting legacies of both the conqueror and the conquered. It was an inheritance that shaped not only my identity but also the way I moved through the world. This realization was both a burden and a responsibility—a call to action that I couldn't ignore.

From that moment on, I dedicated years to unraveling the lost stories of those our family had forgotten, and even more so, the ancestors we didn't know we had. I pored over records, traveled to places that held echoes of our past, and spoke with elders who still carried pieces of our history in their memories. Each discovery became a thread in a larger tapestry, connecting me to the faces and voices that had been erased or ignored for centuries.

The deeper I went, the more I realized how interconnected our stories were—how the people who had fought for their freedom and the ones who had wielded power existed within me, coexisting and battling for space. It was a reconciliation I needed to make, not only for myself but for the generations that came before me. I knew that I couldn't change what happened, but I could reclaim our narratives and honor those who had been silenced.

This exhibition became my way of channeling that reclamation. It is a space where the stories of the forgotten, the resilient, and the powerful could come alive, allowing us to confront and heal the dualities within our own identities. By understanding the journey of our ancestors, I found a way to begin reconciling my place in the world, honoring the complexity of my heritage, and creating a space where others could do the same.

SPELL FOR CALLING THE ANCESTORS

LLAMANDO LOS ANCESTROS

PURPOSE: To invite the presence, guidance, and protection of your ancestors into your space, offering them gratitude and strengthening the ancestral connection. This spell blends elements from Santería and Espiritismo, honoring the Caribbean traditions without the need for blood sacrifice.

INGREDIENTS:

- White candle (purity and protection)
- A bowl of fresh water (a portal for spirits and a cleansing element)
- Dried tobacco leaves (to honor the elders and carry your prayers)
- Palo Santo or sage (for cleansing the space and inviting sacred energy)
- Florida Water (a Caribbean spiritual cologne for blessing and purification)
- Fresh basil leaves (for protection and to open spiritual channels)

- A small plate of offerings (fruits like bananas, mango slices, or coconut shavings)
- A piece of white cloth or handkerchief (to represent peace and clarity)

INSTRUCTIONS:

Prepare Your Space:
Find a quiet place where you can create an altar. Place the white cloth on the surface to form the foundation of your altar. Set the white candle at the center, and surround it with the bowl of water, the dried tobacco leaves, the small plate of fruit offerings, and the fresh basil leaves.

Cleanse the Space:
Light the Palo Santo or sage, and move it around the space in a clockwise motion, cleansing the area of any negative energy. As the smoke rises, say:

"Con el humo sagrado, limpio este lugar,
Para que mis ancestros puedan llegar."
(With the sacred smoke, I cleanse this space,
So my ancestors may arrive.)

Prepare Yourself:
Dip your fingers in the Florida Water and rub it onto your wrists, forehead, and the back of your neck. This prepares you to connect with the spiritual realm. Take a deep breath, feeling your energy shift.

Light the Candle:

Light the white candle and place the dried tobacco leaves in front of it. As the flame flickers, speak your intention:
"Ancestros míos, en esta luz sagrada, los llamo.
Que sus espíritus me rodeen, que su sabiduría me guíe,
Que su protección esté conmigo en este espacio y más allá."
(My ancestors, in this sacred light, I call you.
May your spirits surround me, may your wisdom guide me,
May your protection be with me in this space and beyond.)

Offer the Fruits:
Lift the small plate of fruits towards the flame and the smoke of the incense. With your eyes closed, visualize your ancestors gathering around, accepting your offering. Say:

"Les ofrezco estas frutas, como símbolo de mi gratitud,
Que sus fuerzas me bendigan, y sus caminos me guíen."
(I offer these fruits as a symbol of my gratitude,
May your strength bless me, and your paths guide me.)

Connect and Listen:
Place the fresh basil leaves into the bowl of water, stirring gently with your fingers. This action opens a channel to your ancestors. Sit quietly for a few minutes, breathing deeply, and listen for any messages or feelings that may come. If you

feel a presence or receive guidance, acknowledge it and offer thanks.

Close the Ritual:
To close, say:

> "Gracias, ancestros, por escuchar mi llamado. Sus nombres los honro, sus espíritus los recibo. Que su luz me acompañe, que su amor me sostenga."
> (Thank you, ancestors, for hearing my call. I honor your names, I receive your spirits. May your light accompany me, may your love sustain me.)

Extinguish the Candle:
When you are ready, extinguish the candle by pinching it with wet fingers or using a candle snuffer—never blow it out, as this might dispel the energy. Leave the altar intact for the rest of the day, allowing the water to remain as an offering to your ancestors.

Note: Repeat this spell as needed, especially on special dates like your ancestors' birthdays or significant cultural celebrations. Keep the space and intention pure, and your connection with the ancestors will grow stronger over time.

THE BOHITI TAROT – UNVEILING ANCESTRAL PATHWAYS

My journey into exploring ancestry through art truly began with the creation of the Bohiti Tarot deck. At the time, I was already diving deep into my family history, trying to untangle the complexities of my heritage and uncover the hidden stories of my ancestors. Art had always been a means for me to process and express, but designing the Bohiti Tarot opened an entirely new avenue for connecting with my roots and communicating the spiritual essence of my lineage.

The idea came to me as I was researching Caribbean history and the ancestral practices of the Taíno people. I realized that a tarot deck could serve as a visual and spiritual guide—a bridge between the present and the past, a tool for communion with those who came before me. I envisioned a deck that would incorporate figures from Caribbean history, drawing from the Taíno, Puerto Rican, and Cuban cultures. I wanted the deck to be both an homage to the spirits of the Caribbean and a reclamation of stories that had been erased or distorted through colonization.

As I began sketching out the major arcana, I felt an almost magnetic pull guiding me toward certain figures and symbols. I knew I had to include those whose stories had been silenced—figures from the Taíno resistance against the Spanish, revolutionary leaders from Puerto Rican independence movements, and healers and spiritual leaders who preserved the cultural essence of the islands. Each card became a representation of the complexities of Caribbean history: the resilience of the enslaved, the power of spiritual leaders, and the defiance of political rebels.

The process of designing each card was like opening a portal. I found myself channeling the spirits and energies I was learning about, feeling their presence and their stories flow through me. It was as if they were guiding my hand, helping me bring their images and voices to life. The figures on each card weren't just static representations; they were alive, carrying the weight of the past and the hopes of the future. They told stories of power, of struggle, of love and loss—stories that I realized were embedded in my own DNA.

Creating the Bohiti Tarot was not only an artistic challenge but a deeply spiritual experience. It required me to confront my own position as both a descendant of the colonized and the colonizer. As I drew the conquistadors and the Taíno warriors, I felt the duality within me—this constant push and pull of power, identity, and resistance. I poured these emotions into the deck, hoping that others who engaged with the cards could feel the same sense of reconciliation and understanding.

The more I created, the more I realized how art could be a conduit for ancestral connection. The Bohiti Tarot wasn't just a deck of cards; it was a map, a guide for others like me who were searching for their place in the world, longing to connect with their roots. It became a way for me to reclaim my identity and honor the ancestors who shaped the Caribbean's history, culture, and spiritual practices.

In designing the deck, I felt the boundaries of time dissolve. It was no longer about the past or the present; it was about an ongoing dialogue, a continuum where ancestral wisdom was always accessible, always present. The Bohiti Tarot became my personal invitation to journey deeper into the mysteries of my heritage, to allow art to be the vessel through which I could not only understand my ancestors but also honor and uplift them.

This project set the stage for everything that followed. It was my artistic exploration of ancestry that opened my eyes to the power of reclaiming lost stories and of art as a tool for healing and transformation. The Bohiti Tarot deck was my way of saying: I see you, I honor you, and I invite others to do the same.

FROM THE BOHITI TAROT TO "LA ULTIMA CENA"

After completing the Bohiti Tarot deck, I found myself surrounded by the stories and figures I had brought to life. They felt like companions—ancestors who had guided me through the creation of the deck, helping me channel their power and wisdom. As I continued to explore my artistic practice, I knew I wanted to expand these connections even further, to create a piece that could honor them collectively and challenge the narratives imposed by colonial histories. That's when the concept for "La Ultima Cena" began to take shape.

The Bohiti Tarot had given me a visual and symbolic language to communicate with the past. I had already chosen figures that represented pivotal moments and personas in Caribbean history—heroes, healers, spiritual leaders, warriors, and political revolutionaries. These individuals embodied the resilience, courage, and sacred power of my ancestors. They were the ones who fought for freedom, preserved our cultural traditions, and protected the spirit of the islands. When I envisioned "La Ultima Cena," I knew these same figures would have to be central to its design.

I was inspired by the iconic imagery of The Last Supper, but I wanted to reframe it in a way that reclaimed power and agency for those who had been historically silenced. Rather than using the traditional Christian figures, I decided to bring the Caribbean's own sacred and revolutionary icons to the table—those I had discovered and honored through the Bohiti Tarot. My goal was to create a space where people could sit with their ancestors, commune with their energy, and reflect on the power dynamics that had shaped our history.

Designing "La Ultima Cena" was an immersive process. I began by selecting figures from the deck that I felt were most significant to the concept—those who had represented the strength, resilience, and spirituality of the Caribbean. The Taíno leaders who had resisted Spanish conquest, the spiritual healers who carried the wisdom of our ancestors, the enslaved people who had fought for their freedom, and the political activists who had challenged colonial oppression—all these figures would be seated at this new table, reclaiming their place in history.

As I created the 3D wood cutouts for the piece, I used the imagery from the tarot as my guide. The figures clicked together like puzzle pieces, symbolizing the interconnectedness of our past, present, and future. The act of physically assembling them was a way for me to weave these stories together, bringing them into a unified space where their voices could be heard collectively. Each cutout became more than a representation; it was a vessel of energy, a spirit that invited viewers to engage and reconsider the narratives they had been taught.

In placing these figures at the table, I sought to reclaim the power to choose who we exalt, instead of allowing colonial and religious systems to dictate it. "La Ultima Cena" became a space where we, as descendants, could honor those whose stories were often hidden or erased. It was a way to challenge the idea of divinity that had been imposed upon us, replacing it with our own sacred leaders, healers, and warriors—those who reflected the true essence of Caribbean spirituality and resistance.

The process of bringing these figures from the Bohiti Tarot into "La Ultima Cena" was a powerful experience. It deepened my understanding of the connection between art, spirituality, and ancestry. It felt as though I was not only creating a piece of art but building an altar—a place where the spirits of the Caribbean could be uplifted, honored, and given the space they deserved. By transforming The Last Supper into a gathering of our ancestors, I aimed to create a sacred communion where we, as a community, could sit, reflect, and reclaim the power of our collective history.

"La Ultima Cena" became a living extension of the Bohiti Tarot—an invitation for others to join the dialogue, to sit with the spirits of our past, and to engage in the act of reimagining who holds the power in our stories. It was a way for me to honor those figures, not just through cards, but through a physical and immersive experience where their presence could be felt, seen, and remembered.

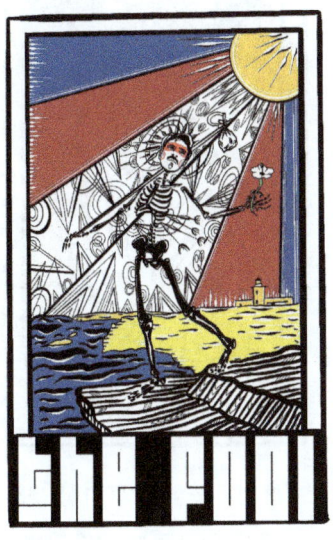

FIGURE: RAFAEL TUFIÑO

THE FOOL IS A CARD OF NEW BEGINNINGS, OPPORTUNITY AND POTENTIAL. JUST LIKE THE YOUNG MAN, YOU ARE AT THE OUTSET OF YOUR JOURNEY, STANDING AT THE CLIFF'S EDGE, AND ABOUT TO TAKE YOUR FIRST STEP INTO THE UNKNOWN. EVEN THOUGH YOU DON'T KNOW EXACTLY WHERE YOU ARE GOING, YOU ARE BEING CALLED TO COMMIT YOURSELF AND FOLLOW YOUR HEART, NO MATTER HOW CRAZY THIS LEAP OF FAITH MIGHT SEEM TO YOU. NOW IS A TIME WHEN YOU NEED TO TRUST WHERE THE UNIVERSE IS TAKING YOU.

RAFAEL TUFIÑO'S PAINTINGS INCLUDED PORTRAITS, LANDSCAPES AND IMAGES OF PUERTO RICAN DAILY LIFE. DURING THE 1950S, HE WAS PART OF THE "GENERACIÓN DE LOS CINCUENTAS" (THE GENERATION OF THE FIFTIES), A GROUP OF ARTISTS WHO WORKED TO CREATE A NEW ARTISTIC STYLE AND AESTHETIC IDENTITY FOR PUERTO RICO.

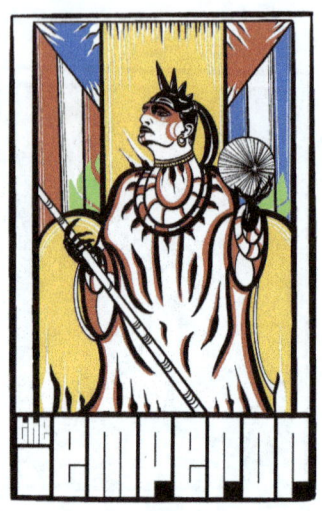

FIGURE: CACIQUE HATÜEY

THE FAMED TAÍNO CACIQUE AS THE EMPEROR HAS VAST SIGNIFICANCE. THE EMPEROR CALLS FOR YOU TO BE FATHERLY, TO PROTECT AND ENSURE STABILITY AND SECURITY FOR THOSE AROUND YOU. THE EMPEROR REPRESENTS A POWERFUL LEADER WHO DEMANDS RESPECT AND AUTHORITY. HIS FIGHT AGAINST THE SPANISH PUSH OF CHRISTIANITY ON THE TAÍNO PROVES THAT THIS CARD NOT ONLY EXEMPLIFIES HIM BUT HIS ANCESTRAL CONNECTION TO LEADERSHIP AS A WHOLE.

"HERE IS THE GOD THE SPANIARDS WORSHIP. FOR THESE THEY FIGHT AND KILL; FOR THESE THEY PERSECUTE US AND THAT IS WHY WE HAVE TO THROW THEM INTO THE SEA... THEY TELL US, THESE TYRANTS, THAT THEY ADORE A GOD OF PEACE AND EQUALITY, AND YET THEY USURP OUR LAND AND MAKE US THEIR SLAVES. THEY SPEAK TO US OF AN IMMORTAL SOUL AND OF THEIR ETERNAL REWARDS AND PUNISHMENTS, AND YET THEY ROB OUR BELONGINGS, SEDUCE OUR WOMEN, VIOLATE OUR DAUGHTERS. INCAPABLE OF MATCHING US IN VALOR, THESE COWARDS COVER THEMSELVES WITH IRON THAT OUR WEAPONS CANNOT BREAK."

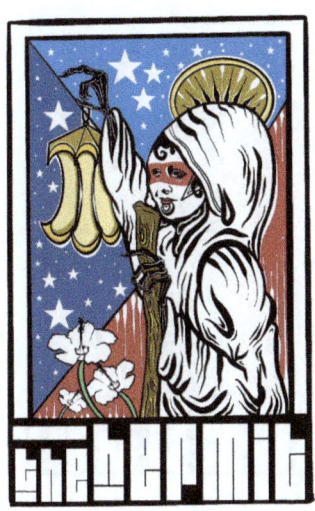

FIGURE: JULIA DE BURGOS

THE HERMIT SHOWS THAT YOU ARE TAKING A BREAK FROM EVERYDAY LIFE TO DRAW YOUR ENERGY AND ATTENTION INWARD AND FIND THE ANSWERS YOU SEEK, DEEP WITHIN YOUR SOUL. YOU REALISE THAT YOUR MOST PROFOUND SENSE OF TRUTH AND KNOWLEDGE IS WITHIN YOURSELF AND NOT IN THE DISTRACTIONS OF THE OUTSIDE WORLD.

YOU LEAVE BEHIND THE MUNDANE TO SET OFF ON A JOURNEY OF SELF-DISCOVERY, LED ONLY BY YOUR INNER WISDOM AND GUIDING LIGHT. NOW IS THE PERFECT TIME TO GO ON A WEEKEND RETREAT OR SACRED PILGRIMAGE, ANYTHING IN WHICH YOU CAN CONTEMPLATE YOUR MOTIVATIONS, PERSONAL VALUES AND PRINCIPLES, AND GET CLOSER TO YOUR AUTHENTIC SELF.

JULIA DE BURGOS GARCÍA (FEBRUARY 17, 1914 – JULY 6, 1953) WAS A PUERTO RICAN POET. AS AN ADVOCATE OF PUERTO RICAN INDEPENDENCE, SHE SERVED AS SECRETARY GENERAL OF THE DAUGHTERS OF FREEDOM, THE WOMEN'S BRANCH OF THE PUERTO RICAN NATIONALIST PARTY. IN FEBRUARY 1953, DURING HER LAST HOSPITALIZATION, SHE WROTE ONE OF HER LAST POEMS, "FAREWELL IN WELFARE ISLAND." IT IS BELIEVED BY HER PEERS TO BE ONE OF THE ONLY POEMS SHE WROTE IN ENGLISH. IN THE POEM SHE FORESHADOWS HER DEATH AND REVEALS AN EVER DARKER CONCEPT OF LIFE.

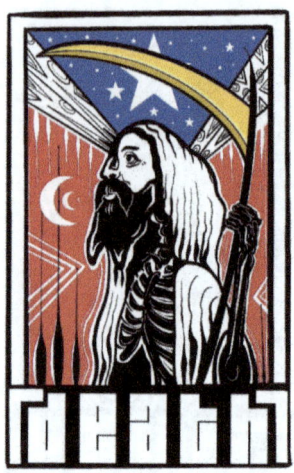

FIGURE: JUAN PONCE DE LEON

After a period of pause and reflection with the Hanged Man, the Death card symbolises the end of a major phase or aspect of your life that you realise is no longer serving you, opening up the possibility of something far more valuable and essential. You must close one door to open another. You need to put the past behind you and part ways, ready to embrace new opportunities and possibilities. It may be difficult to let go of the past, but you will soon see its importance and the promise of renewal and transformation. If you resist these necessary endings, you may experience pain, both emotionally and physically, but if you exercise your imagination and visualise a new possibility, you allow more constructive patterns to emerge.

By the early 1500s, Ponce de León was a top military official in the colonial government of Hispaniola, where he helped crush a rebellion of the native Taíno people. He was authorized to explore the neighboring island of Puerto Rico in 1508 and for serving as the first Governor of Puerto Rico by appointment of the Spanish crown in 1509. While Ponce de León grew quite wealthy from his plantations and mines, he faced an ongoing legal conflict with Diego Columbus, the late Christopher Columbus's son, over the right to govern Puerto Rico. After a long court battle, Columbus replaced Ponce de León as governor in 1511.

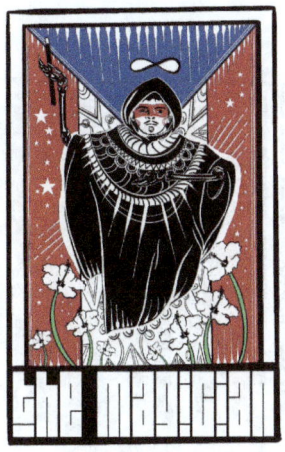

FIGURE: RAFAEL CANCEL MIRANDA

As a master manifestor, the Magician brings you the tools, resources and energy you need to make your dreams come true. Seriously, everything you need right now is at your fingertips. You have the spiritual (fire), physical (earth), mental (air) and emotional (water) resources to manifest your desires. And when you combine them with the energy of the spiritual and earthly realms, you will become a manifestation powerhouse! The key is to bring these tools together synergistically so that the impact of what you create is greater than the separate parts. This is alchemy at its best!

Rafael Cancel Miranda was a poet, political activist, member of the Puerto Rican Nationalist Party and an advocate of Puerto Rican independence. On March 1, 1954, Cancel Miranda and three other Nationalists attacked the United States Capitol building, firing 30 shots and injuring five congressmen.

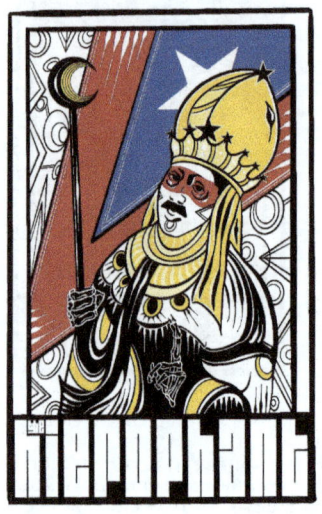

FIGURE: RAFAEL CORDERO

THE HIEROPHANT'S ARRIVAL SUGGESTS YOU ARE FOLLOWING CONVENTION AND STAYING WITHIN THE BOUNDS OF A 'TRIED AND TESTED' MODEL. YOU ARE NOT YET WILLING TO GO OUT ON A LIMB OR OFFER ANY NEW AND INNOVATIVE IDEAS. INSTEAD, YOU ADHERE TO THE KEY PRINCIPLES AND RULES THAT YOU KNOW WILL LEAD TO A SUCCESSFUL RESULT.

RAFAEL CORDERO Y MOLINA (OCTOBER 24, 1790 – JULY 5, 1868), KNOWN AS MAESTRO CORDERO, WAS A SELF-EDUCATED PUERTO RICAN WHO PROVIDED FREE SCHOOLING TO THE CHILDREN OF HIS CITY REGARDLESS OF RACE OR SOCIAL STANDING. HE IS ALSO KNOWN AS THE "FATHER OF PUBLIC EDUCATION IN PUERTO RICO".

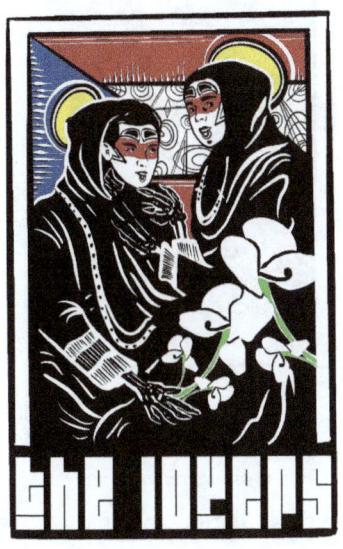

FIGURES: OSCAR COLLAZO AND GRISELIO TORRESOLA

THE LOVERS CARD REPRESENTS GETTING CLEAR ABOUT YOUR VALUES AND BELIEFS. YOU ARE FIGURING OUT WHAT YOU STAND FOR AND YOUR PHILOSOPHY. HAVING GONE THROUGH THE INDOCTRINATION OF THE HIEROPHANT, YOU ARE NOW READY TO ESTABLISH YOUR BELIEF SYSTEM AND DECIDE WHAT IS AND WHAT IS NOT ESSENTIAL TO YOU.

TWO PUERTO RICAN PRO-INDEPENDENCE PROPONENTS, OSCAR COLLAZO AND GRISELIO TORRESOLA, ATTEMPTED TO ASSASSINATE PRESIDENT HARRY S. TRUMAN. TORRESOLA AND COLLAZO BELONGED TO THE PUERTO RICAN NATIONALIST PARTY, WHICH SOUGHT TO GAIN INDEPENDENCE FROM THE UNITED STATES. I THOUGHT THEY WOULD BE PERFECT FOR THE CARD, SHOWCASING A STRONG FAITH IN THEIR BELIEF SYSTEM.

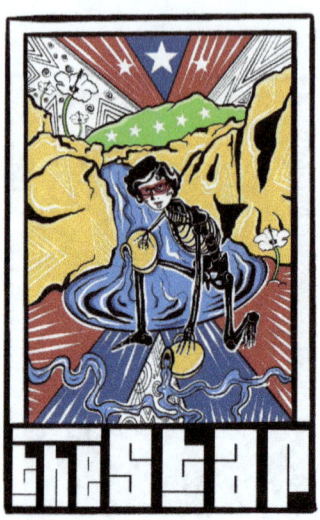

FIGURE: OLGA ALBIZU

As the Star follows the Tower card in the Tarot, it comes as a welcome reprieve after a period of destruction and turmoil. You have endured many challenges and stripped yourself bare of any limiting beliefs that have previously held you back. You are realising your core essence, who you are beneath all the layers. No matter what life throws your way, you know that you are always connected to the Divine and pure loving energy. You hold a new sense of self, a new appreciation for the core of your Being.

Albizu was born and raised in Puerto Rico, where she studied painting with the Spanish painter Esteban Vicente from 1943 to 1947. She received a B.A. from the University of Puerto Rico in 1946. In 1948 she moved to New York City on a fellowship for post-graduate work at the Art Students League, where she studied under Morris Kantor, Carl Holty, and Vaclav Vytlacil. She also studied with Hans Hofmann and subsequently became his apprentice. After that, she did further studies in Europe at the Académie de la Grande Chaumière in Paris and the Accademia di Belle Arti in Florence. Later, she spent a year painting in the Provence, as painters such as Van Gogh and Cézanne had done before her.

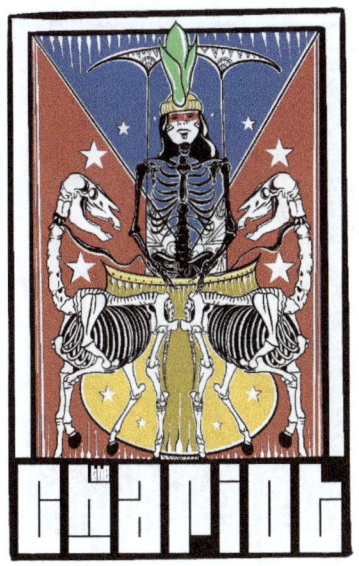

FIGURE: AGÜEYBANÁ II

WHEN THE CHARIOT APPEARS IN A TAROT READING, TAKE IT AS A SIGN OF ENCOURAGEMENT. YOU HAVE SET YOUR OBJECTIVES AND ARE NOW CHANNELLING YOUR INNER POWER WITH A FIERCE DEDICATION TO BRING THEM TO FRUITION. WHEN YOU APPLY DISCIPLINE, COMMITMENT AND WILLPOWER TO ACHIEVE YOUR GOALS, YOU WILL SUCCEED. NOW ISN'T THE TIME TO BE PASSIVE IN THE HOPE THAT THINGS WILL WORK OUT IN YOUR FAVOUR. TAKE FOCUSED ACTION AND STICK TO THE COURSE, NO MATTER WHAT CHALLENGES MAY COME YOUR WAY – BECAUSE, BELIEVE ME, THERE WILL BE CHALLENGES.

AGÜEYBANÁ II, BORN GÜEYBANÁ AND ALSO KNOWN AS AGÜEYBANÁ EL BRAVO, WAS ONE OF THE TWO PRINCIPAL AND MOST POWERFUL TAÍNO CACIQUES OF THE BORIKÉN WHEN THE SPANIARDS FIRST ARRIVED IN PUERTO RICO ON NOVEMBER 19, 1493.

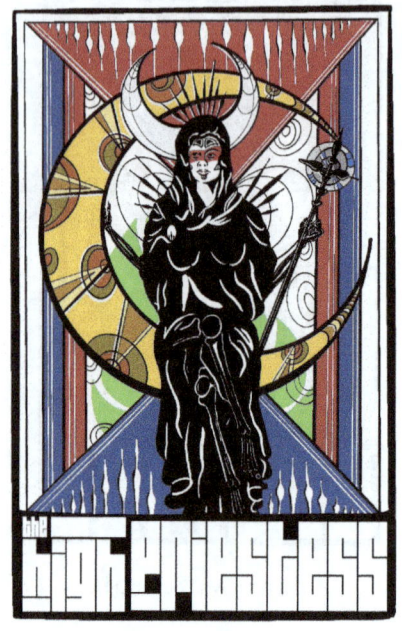

FIGURE: CACIQUE YUIZA

THE HIGH PRIESTESS SIGNIFIES SPIRITUAL ENLIGHTENMENT, INNER ILLUMINATION, DIVINE KNOWLEDGE AND WISDOM. SHE SHOWS UP IN YOUR TAROT READINGS WHEN THE VEIL BETWEEN YOU AND THE UNDERWORLD IS THIN, AND YOU HAVE THE OPPORTUNITY TO ACCESS THE KNOWLEDGE DEEP WITHIN YOUR SOUL.

THE LEGEND IS THAT THE NAME LOIZA WAS THAT OF A TAINO WOMAN, CHIEF LOIZA OR YUISA, WHO GOVERNED A TERRITORY CALLED JAYMANIO IN THE MARGINS OF THE CAYRABON RIVER NOW NAMED THE RIO GRANDE DE LOIZA.

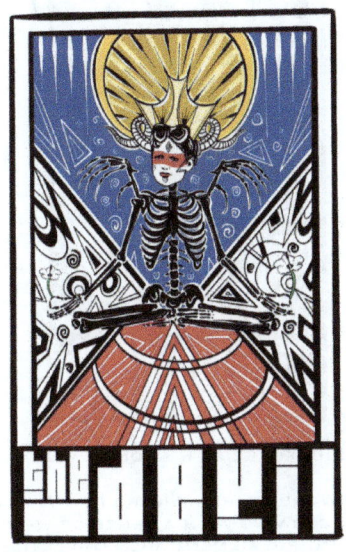

FIGURE: LOLA RODRIGUEZ DE TIÓ

THE DEVIL CARD REPRESENTS YOUR SHADOW (OR DARKER) SIDE AND THE NEGATIVE FORCES THAT CONSTRAIN YOU AND HOLD YOU BACK FROM BEING THE BEST VERSION OF YOURSELF. YOU MAY BE AT THE EFFECT OF NEGATIVE HABITS, DEPENDENCIES, BEHAVIOURS, THOUGHT PATTERNS, RELATIONSHIPS, AND ADDICTIONS. YOU HAVE FOUND YOURSELF TRAPPED BETWEEN THE SHORT-TERM PLEASURE YOU RECEIVE AND THE LONGER-TERM PAIN YOU EXPERIENCE. JUST AS THE LOVERS CARD SPEAKS TO DUALITY AND CHOICE, SO TOO DOES THE DEVIL; HOWEVER, WITH THE DEVIL, YOU ARE CHOOSING THE PATH OF INSTANT GRATIFICATION, EVEN IF IT IS AT THE EXPENSE OF YOUR LONG-TERM WELL-BEING

LOLA RODRÍGUEZ DE TIÓ, (SEPTEMBER 14, 1843 – NOVEMBER 10, 1924), WAS THE FIRST PUERTO RICAN-BORN WOMAN POET TO ESTABLISH HERSELF A REPUTATION AS A GREAT POET THROUGHOUT ALL OF LATIN AMERICA. A BELIEVER IN WOMEN'S RIGHTS, SHE WAS ALSO COMMITTED TO THE ABOLITION OF SLAVERY AND THE INDEPENDENCE OF PUERTO RICO.

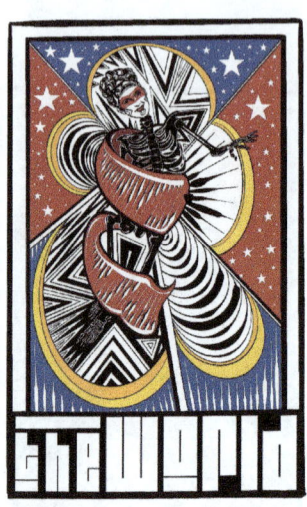

FIGURE: FELISA RINCÓN DE GUATIER

When the World card appears in a Tarot reading, you are glowing with a sense of wholeness, achievement, fulfilment and completion. A long-term project, period of study, relationship or career has come full circle, and you are now revelling in the sense of closure and accomplishment. This card could represent graduation, a marriage, the birth of a child or achieving a long-held dream or aspiration. You have finally accomplished your goal or purpose. Everything has come together, and you are in the right place, doing the right thing, achieving what you have envisioned. You feel whole and complete.

Rincón de Gautier was a firm believer in the women's right to vote and was an active participant in the suffragist movement, motivating many women to register. When the law allowing women to vote was passed, Rincón de Gautier was the fifth woman to officially register. In 1932, she joined the Liberal Party of Puerto Rico, which believed in Puerto Rico's independence, and was named representative by the party's president Antonio R. Barceló. Motivated by the political ideas of Luis Muñoz Marín, she left the Liberal Party and in 1938 helped organize the Popular Democratic Party of Puerto Rico. She was the first woman to be elected as the Mayor of a capital city in The Americas.

THE DEEPER SYMBOLISM OF "LA ÚLTIMA CENA" – THE TAROT HAND AND ANCESTRAL NARRATIVE

In "La Ultima Cena," each card is strategically placed not just as a representation of its tarot meaning but as a profound connection between the figure's historical legacy, their positioning in the seating chart, and the overall narrative of Caribbean resistance, resilience, and transformation. This hand of tarot cards is not simply a random selection; it is a deliberate orchestration of ancestral energies and stories that, when viewed as a whole, weave together a powerful commentary on the historical and spiritual journey of the Caribbean.

THE EMPEROR IN JESUS'S SPACE – CACIQUE HATÜEY

Placed in the most central and influential space, traditionally occupied by Jesus, The Emperor represented by Cacique Hatüey becomes the focal point of the table. The Emperor is a card of authority, leadership, and power. Hatüey, as the first known leader to resist Spanish colonization, holds the seat of the savior figure—reframing the idea of sacrifice as a choice for liberation rather than a submission to oppression. His placement here honors him as the spiritual leader and protector of the Caribbean people, positioning him as the symbolic heart of resistance. This space represents the epicenter of the table's power dynamics, and it speaks to the centrality of leadership and resistance in reclaiming identity.

The Hermit in John's Space – Julia de Burgos

The Hermit, occupying John's space, is represented by Julia de Burgos, whose deep introspection and poetic vision guide Puerto Rican cultural identity. In the traditional Last Supper, John is known as the closest disciple, the beloved one who remains faithful. The Hermit's spiritual journey mirrors de Burgos's own solitary path, where her poetry became a vessel for truth, self-discovery, and the fight for independence. Positioned next to the central figure of Hatüey, she is the faithful seeker whose voice calls for liberation, making her a crucial support to the Emperor's cause. Her position underscores the importance of internal reflection in fueling external change.

Death in Judas's Space – Juan Ponce de León

In the space traditionally reserved for Judas, Death is symbolized by Juan Ponce de León, the Spanish conquistador who governed Puerto Rico. Judas's role as the betrayer is inverted here; the Death card signifies the transformative power needed to confront and overcome historical wrongs. Ponce de León's presence in this seat forces a reckoning with the past—a confrontation with colonialism's legacy and the inevitable change required to dismantle its structures. This card serves as a bridge, signaling the shift from oppressive rule to the potential rebirth of a liberated identity. It emphasizes that sometimes, betrayal (or the confrontation with uncomfortable truths) is necessary for transformation.

THE HIGH PRIESTESS IN MATTHEW'S SPACE – CACIQUE YUIZA

The High Priestess occupies Matthew's space and is represented by Cacique Yuiza, one of the few recorded female Taíno leaders. The High Priestess is a card of intuition, mystery, and spiritual authority, aligning with Yuiza's role as a leader who maintained spiritual and cultural traditions amidst colonization. Positioned on the side of the Emperor, she acts as the spiritual advisor, connecting the physical fight for sovereignty to the metaphysical realms. Her presence in this space highlights the vital role of Indigenous women as keepers of knowledge and wisdom, essential in guiding and supporting revolutionary efforts. She embodies the spiritual backbone of the table.

THE FOOL IN THOMAS'S SPACE – RAFAEL TUFIÑO

Placed in Thomas's space, traditionally occupied by the doubter, The Fool is represented by Rafael Tufiño. The Fool is a card of new beginnings and the courage to leap into the unknown. Tufiño, as an artist who redefined Puerto Rican visual identity, embodies this spirit of bold transformation. In a space associated with skepticism, The Fool challenges doubt and uncertainty by embracing the unknown, suggesting that to move forward, one must have the courage to step beyond fear and reshape reality. The positioning reinforces that art and culture are integral to pushing past colonial narratives and imagining a future that reclaims and celebrates identity.

THE STAR IN PETER'S SPACE – OLGA ALBIZU

The Star occupies Peter's space and is represented by Olga Albizu. Peter, the rock upon which the church is built, symbolizes faith and stability. Albizu's contributions to abstract expressionism and her elevation of Puerto Rican culture serve as the guiding light of this position. The Star card brings hope and inspiration, aligning with her transformative influence in the art world. Her placement as Peter signifies that the foundation of cultural identity rests on visionary efforts—those who use their talents to illuminate and guide communities forward. Her light shines as a beacon for future generations to follow, illustrating the transformative power of art.

THE LOVERS IN JAMES AND ANDREW'S SPACE – OSCAR COLLAZO AND GRISELIO TORRESOLA

In the dual space of James and Andrew, The Lovers is represented by Oscar Collazo and Griselio Torresola. The Lovers signify choices, unity, and partnership. Their attempt to assassinate President Truman was an act of commitment to Puerto Rico's independence, showing their unity in the face of oppression. Positioned as a pair, they symbolize the duality of struggle and the importance of solidarity in the fight for freedom. Their placement represents the necessity of partnerships and alliances in the larger battle for liberation, emphasizing the collective strength needed to overcome colonial powers.

THE WORLD IN BARTHOLOMEW'S SPACE – FELISA RINCÓN DE GAUTIER

The World, represented by Felisa Rincón de Gautier, occupies Bartholomew's space, traditionally linked to expansion and mission work. The World card signifies fulfillment, wholeness, and accomplishment. As the first woman mayor of a capital city in the Americas,

Rincón de Gautier's legacy reflects these qualities. Her presence in this space highlights the importance of expanding opportunities and creating a unified vision for progress. It symbolizes the completion of cycles and the realization of long-term goals, advocating for a comprehensive vision of freedom that includes political, social, and gender equality.

THE HIEROPHANT IN JAMES MAJOR'S SPACE – RAFAEL CORDERO

The Hierophant, represented by Rafael Cordero, sits in James Major's space. The Hierophant signifies tradition, knowledge, and spiritual guidance. Cordero's role as an educator who championed public education aligns with this symbolism, advocating for the preservation of cultural and educational values as a foundation for identity. Positioned here, he serves as the moral compass of the table, reinforcing the importance of education in maintaining cultural heritage and ensuring the empowerment of future generations.

THE MAGICIAN IN PHILIP'S SPACE – RAFAEL CANCEL MIRANDA

The Magician in Philip's space is symbolized by Rafael Cancel Miranda, a political activist and nationalist. The Magician represents manifestation, skill, and transformation—apt for Cancel Miranda, who actively worked to bring about political change. Positioned here, The

Magician signifies the power of activism and the ability to harness one's talents to create tangible outcomes. This placement serves as a reminder that action and intention are critical in shaping history and reclaiming sovereignty.

THE CHARIOT IN THADDEUS'S SPACE – AGÜEYBANÁ II

The Chariot, symbolized by Agüeybaná II, takes Thaddeus's space. Known for his leadership during early Spanish encounters, Agüeybaná II embodies the Chariot's themes of willpower, determination, and victory. This placement emphasizes the relentless pursuit of autonomy and the strength required to navigate challenges. As a figure of resistance, Agüeybaná II's presence reinforces the importance of courage and unity in the face of colonization, showing that the path to freedom requires both strategy and resolve.

THE DEVIL IN SIMON'S SPACE – LOLA RODRÍGUEZ DE TIÓ

In Simon's space, The Devil is represented by Lola Rodríguez de Tió. The Devil card explores the struggle with power and control, making Rodríguez de Tió's position here symbolic of the duality inherent in the fight for liberation. While she fought against colonial rule and advocated for independence, the card suggests the shadows and complexities of these battles—the ways in which power can be both oppressive and liberatory. Her position highlights the necessity of confronting and transcending these shadows.

THE HAND AS A WHOLE: A SYMBOLIC ORCHESTRATION

The tarot hand in "La Ultima Cena" serves as a comprehensive journey through Caribbean resistance and identity formation. Each card not only reflects an individual's story but also builds on the collective narrative of transformation, struggle, and resilience. The figures chosen—ranging from spiritual leaders and artists to revolutionaries and educators—create a tapestry that connects the physical, spiritual, and cultural dimensions of liberation.

As a whole, this hand is a call to action: a reminder that freedom is not a singular moment but an ongoing process requiring both internal and external work. The spread symbolizes the balance between leadership (Hatüey as The Emperor), introspection (de Burgos as The Hermit), action (Cancel Miranda as The Magician), and unity (Collazo and Torresola as The Lovers). It suggests that to reclaim identity and autonomy, a holistic approach that integrates spiritual wisdom, cultural expression, political action, and collective solidarity is essential.

This hand, therefore, is both a reflection and a guide—showing that the journey of liberation, while filled with challenges (Death, The Devil), is ultimately one of fulfillment (The World) and renewal (The Star). It is a powerful reminder that the Caribbean story is one of resilience, rooted in a deep ancestral connection that continues to guide and inspire.

Hymn for the Ancestral Trinity

O sacred trinity of grace,
Guide us through this time and space.
Father's hands that built and strayed,
Mother's love that shaped and swayed.
Child who walks the path alone,
In your strength, we find our own.

Ancestor's breath and spirit's fire,
Lift us up, take us higher.
In loss, in love, and life's embrace,
We bow before your holy face.
Teach us wisdom, teach us might,
Guard our hearts and grant us sight.

Blessed voices, call us near,
In our souls, let truth appear.
Guide our steps and light our way,
Through the night and into day.
In your name, we find our plea,
Ancestral trinity, set us free.

THE TRIPTIC OF "CHILD[LESS]," "EL PADRE," AND "LA MADRE" – AN ANCESTRAL TRINITY

In the heart of the exhibition stands a powerful triptych composed of "Child[Less]," "El Padre," and "La Madre." These three pieces are not just artworks; they form a sacred trinity—a reflection of the complexities of family, identity, and the profound influence of ancestry. This triptych is imbued with personal, historical, and spiritual significance, merging the sacred and the profane in a meditation on lineage, loss, and reclamation. At its feet, a prayer bench is positioned, inviting viewers to engage not merely as observers but as active participants in an act of reverence and introspection.

"CHILD[LESS]" – THE SELF-PORTRAIT OF A CHILDLESS MOTHER

"Child[Less]" is my self-portrait, a deeply personal representation of my experience with loss, motherhood, and identity. This work captures the essence of being a mother who, despite the absence of her child, carries the imprint of motherhood in every aspect of her being. The title itself is intentional—a confrontation with the idea of "childless," challenging the perception of motherhood as something defined solely by physical presence. It asserts that my identity as a mother exists even when my child does not live with me, and even in the face of miscarriage, abortion, and estrangement.

In this piece, I use concentric rings to symbolize my abortions and miscarriages. These rings are reminiscent of the sacred halos often seen in religious art, turning the pain of loss into something divine, an element of my identity. The wax I chose—once fluid and malleable—is now solidified, capturing the impression of a life that is both formed and fragmented. It's deliberate; the wax signifies how life can become rigid and marked by experiences, yet still holds the potential for transformation.

I chose to place "Child[Less]" at the center of the triptych for a reason. In the context of the Holy Trinity, it assumes the role of the Son, the figure through whom suffering and sacrifice are channeled. But in my reimagined trinity, the traditional patriarchal symbol of the Son is replaced by the figure of a mother—a childless mother who, despite her pain, continues to exist in the world. This inversion challenges viewers to rethink their understanding of sacrifice and sanctity, and to recognize the holiness present in all forms of motherhood.

By positioning a prayer bench directly in front of "Child[Less]," I'm inviting the viewer to bow—not to an external savior, but to the embodiment of maternal strength and resilience. The act of bowing, which is traditionally reserved for divine figures, is now directed toward a childless mother. It's a radical gesture that compels viewers to honor the overlooked, the forgotten, and the misinterpreted aspects of motherhood. It's a statement that the sacred resides in the experiences of loss just as much as it does in creation.

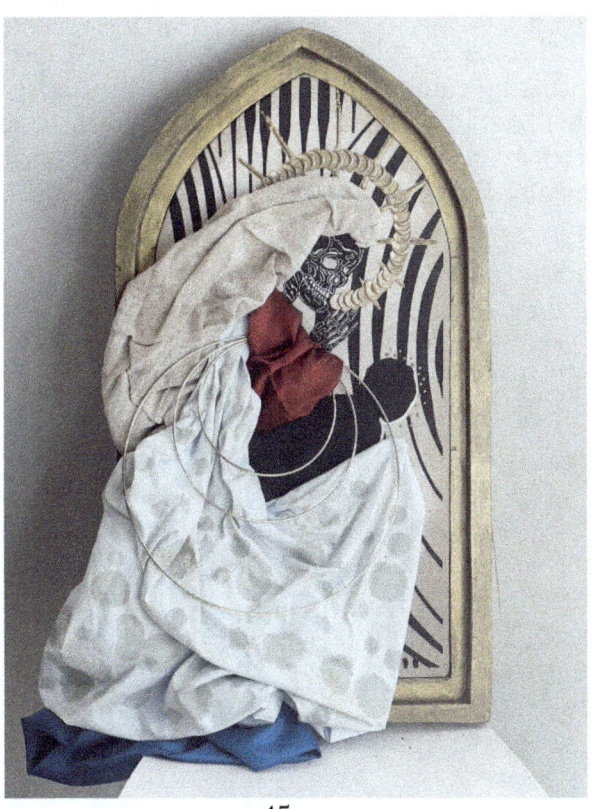

"EL PADRE" – THE ABSENCE OF A FATHER

To the right of "Child[Less]," I placed "El Padre," a portrait of my father, whose presence in my life was both real and distant. This piece represents the figure of the Father within the trinity, yet it subverts traditional expectations of paternal authority. My father's image is rendered with a sense of detachment, reflecting a life spent in constant motion—an aircraft mechanic who traveled extensively, physically present but often emotionally distant. The portrayal captures a man shaped by his own history, by a lineage of conquest and displacement, and the ripple effect of those histories on our relationship.

"El Padre" explores the theme of absence within presence, a concept deeply rooted in colonial legacies where familial bonds were often fractured by displacement, migration, and the pursuit of survival. My father's absence in my life isn't just a void but an active presence that continues to shape who I am, much like the distant influence of colonization shapes the cultural identities of the colonized. This piece challenges viewers to reconsider the traditional image of the father—not as an omnipotent figure, but as one whose power lies in the ways he has shaped his child's understanding of both presence and absence.

The placement of "El Padre" to the right of "Child[Less]" reflects a balance within the trinity, connecting my experience as a childless mother with the figure of a father who, while significant, remains elusive. The prayer bench before this arrangement becomes a space not only to honor the mother but to acknowledge the impact of fathers who may be physically present but emotionally distant.

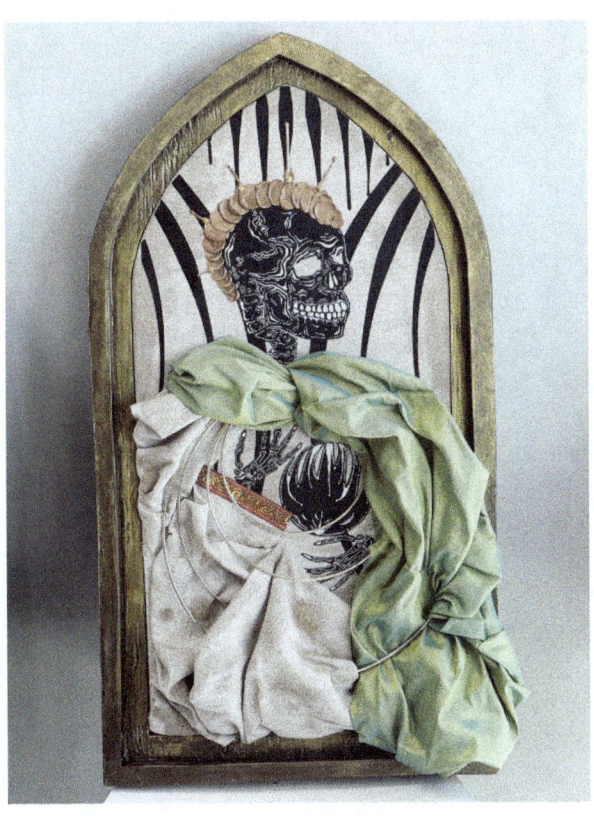

"La Madre" – The Duality of Love and Control

To the left of "Child[Less]" is "La Madre," my portrayal of my mother, a figure who embodied both love and dominance. In the context of the Holy Trinity, "La Madre" takes the place of the Holy Spirit, the maternal, nurturing energy that connects and sustains. My mother's presence in this triptych is complex—she is portrayed as royal and authoritative, embodying the duality of being both loving and controlling. This duality reflects my lifelong navigation of her influence, a journey of reconciling the nurturing care I received with the oppressive expectations and control that came with it.

In traditional religious iconography, the Holy Spirit is often depicted as the invisible force that breathes life into creation. In this reimagining, my mother becomes that force—a presence that is both life-giving and suffocating, shaping my sense of identity and self-worth. The regal portrayal of "La Madre" emphasizes the power dynamics within familial relationships, particularly between mothers and daughters, and the ways in which these dynamics can shape our understanding of ourselves.

By situating "La Madre" to the left of "Child[Less]," the triptych balances the maternal and paternal energies, centering my self-portrait as the focal point. My mother's gaze, like my father's, is directed toward the central figure, creating a dynamic interplay between the three pieces that reflects the push and pull of familial influence.

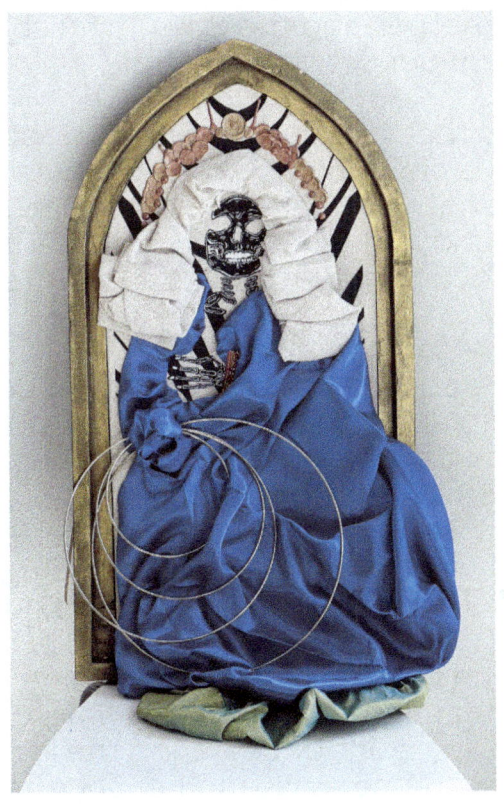

THE PRAYER BENCH: BOWING TO THE TRINITY OF ANCESTRAL INFLUENCE

The prayer bench before the triptych serves as an altar—a space where viewers are invited to kneel and engage in an act of reverence. However, rather than directing their prayers to an external deity, viewers are prompted to honor the complexities of family, the strength of the childless mother, and the ways in which these ancestral influences shape identity.

Bowing to the childless mother is an act of radical reverence. It demands acknowledgment of the strength and sanctity found in loss, in absence, and in the reclamation of identity. The prayer bench transforms the exhibition space into a sacred site, where the maternal experience, so often dismissed or misunderstood, becomes the focus of devotion. It is a call to recognize the sanctity of all forms of motherhood and to bow to the resilience of those who navigate the complexities of identity within and beyond their familial ties.

THE TRINITY AS A SYMBOLIC HAND

The triptych forms a reimagined trinity, challenging the traditional Holy Trinity of Father, Son, and Holy Spirit by centering the lived experiences of the artist and her ancestors. This symbolic hand shifts the focus from divine figures to those who occupy the everyday—those whose stories are marked by complexity, struggle, and resilience. It becomes a trinity of humanity, one that honors the interconnectedness of identity, ancestry, and legacy.

As a whole, the triptych and its accompanying prayer bench invite viewers into a space of reflection, where they are encouraged to confront their own familial dynamics, to honor the stories of loss and survival that shape their identity, and to bow in reverence to the sacredness of their own ancestral lineage. This hand of the trinity, therefore, is not about worshiping a distant god; it is about honoring the godliness within the everyday, the sanctity of the human experience, and the strength found in the untold stories of those who came before us.

SPELL FOR CONNECTING TO THE IRON CROSSES: "EL PESO DE LA CONVERSIÓN"

This spell is intended to establish a connection with the iron crosses of "El Peso de la Conversión," invoking the energy of transformation, ancestral resilience, and the weight of faith that has been carried and reclaimed. The crosses, forged from iron, symbolize the strength needed to navigate the dualities of faith and oppression. Use this spell to align your spirit with the energy of the ancestors who transformed their burdens into strength.

MATERIALS NEEDED:

- A small bowl of sea salt (to cleanse)
- A black candle (for grounding and protection)
- A white candle (for clarity and transformation)
- Dried sage or palo santo (to purify the space)
- A small piece of iron or metal (to represent the crosses)
- Water infused with herbs like rosemary, bay leaf, or basil (for spiritual strength)

INSTRUCTIONS:

Prepare the Space:
Find a quiet place where you can be undisturbed. Cleanse the area by burning sage or palo santo, allowing the smoke to purify the space and your spirit. As you do this, say:
"Smoke of sage (or palo santo), purify this space. Cleanse the air and all who dwell within it. Ancestors, draw near, your presence I embrace."

Set the Iron in the Center:
Place the piece of iron or metal in the center of your space, symbolizing the iron crosses. Light the black candle to one side of the iron and the white candle on the other side. These candles represent the balance of light and shadow, faith and burden.

Salt and Water Ritual:
Sprinkle sea salt in a circle around the iron. As you pour water infused with herbs over your hands, envision the strength of the iron crosses flowing through your veins. Say:

> "Iron forged in fire, crosses borne in pain,
> Ancestral strength, through time, sustain.
> Water pure, and salt of sea,
> Ground my soul, connect me to thee."

Chant of the Crosses:
Close your eyes and take three deep breaths, feeling the energy of the space and the iron in front of you. Visualize the iron crosses standing

tall, carrying the weight of faith, and transforming it into resilience. With each breath, imagine yourself drawing closer to that strength. Chant:

> "Iron crosses, weight of truth,
> Ancestral burden carried through.
> With faith renewed, and spirit whole,
> I honor the path, and I claim my soul."

Pouring the Water:
Pour a small amount of the herb-infused water over the iron piece, letting it flow like the ancestral stories of transformation and reclamation. Visualize the water cleansing the crosses, lifting the weight of past burdens, and transforming them into a source of power and strength. Say:

> "By water's flow and iron's might,
> I cleanse the past, I claim the light.
> Ancestors, guide me, as I stand tall,
> With every step, I break the thrall."

Closing the Spell:
Allow the candles to burn for a few more moments, then extinguish them, starting with the black candle and then the white, acknowledging the balance of shadow and light. As you do this, say:

> "Crosses of iron, burdens transformed,
> In your weight, my power is born.

Guide my steps as I walk this plane,
With each breath, I rise again."

Final Blessing:
Take a moment to bow your head, placing your hands over your heart. Feel the energy of the iron crosses and their message of transformation fill your being. When ready, say:

"With the weight of the cross, and the strength of the past,
I walk with my ancestors, firm and steadfast.
El Peso de la Conversión, my spirit entwined,
In iron's embrace, my power I find."

Take a deep breath and open your eyes. The spell is complete. Leave the iron piece as an offering or keep it as a talisman, reminding you of the strength you carry from those who came before you.

HYMN FOR THE CRUCIFIED

Oh, those who bear the weight of chains,
Who carry wounds and scars of pain,
Your hands and feet, pierced and torn,
In you, the light of truth is born.

For every lash and every cry,
For every tear that leaves the eye,
Your suffering, a song of grace,
A fire that burns in every place.

Lifted high upon the tree,
A symbol of our agony.
Yet in your wounds, we find our might,
Through darkest days and endless night.

Oh, crucified, our hearts are near,
We hold your strength, we feel your fear.
But in the shadow of the cross,
We rise again, despite the loss.

We bow before your sacred pain,
For through your death, we rise again.
May your spirit guide our way,
Through every night and every day.

Blessed are those who stand so high,
Whose spirits soar, though bodies die.
In your name, we lift our cry,

Oh crucified, you never die.

May your courage be our guide,
Through the storm and rising tide.
In your memory, we remain,
In life, in death, we break the chain.

THE WEIGHT OF FAITH – "EL PESO DE LA CONVERSIÓN"

Suspended against the wall, twenty iron crosses hang like heavy memories, each held up by two nails. Their presence is commanding, inviting viewers to confront the duality of faith as both an instrument of oppression and a symbol of resilience. This installation is not merely decorative; it serves as a deliberate meditation on the weight of history, faith, and the power of reclamation, exploring how beliefs have been imposed, transformed, and ultimately reclaimed by those who have carried these burdens.

The decision to use two nails for each cross is significant. It evokes the imagery of crucifixion, but with a crucial difference. While the traditional narrative of crucifixion is one of submission and sacrifice, the use of two nails here reclaims that narrative. These nails anchor and stabilize each cross, symbolizing the agency and strength of those who faced the imposition of faith and chose to redefine its meaning. The nails secure the crosses in place, asserting ownership over the symbol and its history.

Iron, the material I selected for these crosses, carries profound meaning. It is resilient, strong, and enduring—much like the spirit of my ancestors who survived forced conversion, enslavement, and the attempted erasure of their spiritual beliefs. Iron also recalls the memory of shackles and chains, transforming it into a symbol that speaks to both resilience and the history of subjugation. By using iron, I aim to honor the strength of those who came before me, acknowledging both the pain and the power that comes from transforming these burdens into sources of resilience.

The hemp twine binding each cross adds another layer of symbolism. Hemp is an ancient, durable material associated with connection and grounding, representing the ways in which my ancestors held onto their beliefs and practices, even as they were forced to adapt to a new faith. Wrapping the crosses with hemp twine evokes the act of binding together fragmented histories, weaving resilience through time. The twine holds the iron in place, echoing the persistence of cultural memory and the ways in which traditions, even when forced underground, find ways to survive and evolve.

Each cross is further sealed with a Bohiti gold wax stamp—a mark of ancestral power and authenticity. The Bohiti wax seal represents the spiritual authority of the Taíno bohiti, or shaman, and serves as a sign of reclamation. By sealing each cross, I affirm that these symbols, once tools of control, have been transformed into vessels of ancestral strength. The gold wax is a reminder of the sacredness of this transformation, a sign that these crosses are no longer objects of oppression but emblems of empowerment.

The crosses are displayed in an undulating formation, like a wave or a winding path. This arrangement represents the complex journey of faith and identity—how it is not a linear path but a twisting, evolving process that each individual must navigate. As viewers move through the installation, they are forced to interact with the crosses at various heights—some hanging low, nearly within reach, others positioned higher, requiring them to look up. This physical engagement mirrors the journey my ancestors faced as they navigated conversion, adaptation, and reclamation. The viewer's movement—whether they bow beneath the lower crosses or find their way around—symbolizes the choices faced by those before me: to submit, resist, or transform their circumstances.

The weight of faith is not just a historical burden; it is something I carry personally. The tension of navigating my identity as a Caribbean person, with ancestors of Indigenous, African, and European descent, is one I have felt deeply. This installation is my way of grappling with that weight, of confronting and reclaiming it. The iron crosses become a visual manifestation of that tension, anchored by nails and held together by the twine, which represent the choices faced by my ancestors—to submit, to resist, or to transform. The two nails, the binding twine, and the wax seal all work together to symbolize agency, strength, and reclamation.

As viewers walk through the installation, they engage with the weight of faith and history themselves. The placement of the crosses forces them to confront the legacy of conversion, to feel the presence of each nail, the texture of the hemp twine, and the significance of the gold wax seal. These elements create a balancing act, holding the cross steady while reminding the viewer of the choices that anchored and shaped faith across generations. This interaction is a reminder that faith and identity are dynamic, lived experiences, molded by struggle, adaptation, and resilience.

The installation transforms the gallery into a site of reflection, where viewers are invited to confront their own beliefs and inherited histories. "El Peso de la Conversión" is not just about acknowledging the past; it is about transforming it. It is an opportunity to understand that while the crosses—and the faith they represent—were once used to impose and oppress, they are now reclaimed as symbols of ancestral strength. The twine, wax seal, and nails—once symbols of subjugation—become tools of stabilization and empowerment.

This installation becomes a place of healing, a call to recognize the weight we carry and to transform it into a source of strength. It invites viewers to engage, reflect, and honor the resilience that has been passed down through generations, reminding them that the burdens of history can be borne with dignity and redefined into sources of power.

THE INVERSION OF FAITH – CRUCIFIXIÓN DE LA INDIGNA

Twelve crosses hang suspended from the ceiling in my installation "Crucifixión de la Indigna," each of them upside down and crafted from clear acrylic. The crosses vary in size, creating a visually striking composition that immediately confronts the viewer with the complex layers of symbolism inherent in their form and presentation. The number twelve, the use of clear acrylic, and the choice to invert the crosses all carry specific meanings, woven together to convey a narrative of resilience, faith, and the weight of imposed belief systems.

The number twelve is deliberate and rich with significance. In Christian theology, twelve is the number of apostles who spread the teachings of Christ. It also symbolizes completeness, authority, and divine order. However, in "Crucifixión de la Indigna," the twelve crosses do not simply reference the apostles; they symbolize the cycles of faith and power, as well as the perpetuation of religious influence and control over generations. By using twelve, I am addressing the ways in which belief systems are upheld, institutionalized, and cyclically enforced, while simultaneously suggesting a way to break that cycle through reclamation and reinterpretation.

The use of clear acrylic is equally intentional. Acrylic, a modern and synthetic material, is both strong and transparent. Its clarity invites viewers to see through the traditional structure of the cross, suggesting that faith, as it has been imposed upon colonized people, is not as solid or opaque as it may seem. The transparency of the acrylic crosses serves as a metaphor for revealing hidden histories and truths. It invites the viewer to look beyond the imposed structure of Christianity and to recognize the potential for reinterpretation and reclamation of faith. By using a material that allows light to pass through, I challenge the traditional perception of the cross as a heavy, immovable symbol, instead presenting it as something that can be re-envisioned, deconstructed, and reinterpreted.

The crosses in "Crucifixión de la Indigna" are hung upside down, and this inversion is central to the work's meaning. Traditionally, the upside-down cross is associated with St. Peter, one of the twelve apostles. According to Christian lore, Peter chose to be crucified upside down because he felt unworthy to die in the same manner as Jesus. In this installation, the upside-down crosses echo this act of humility but also serve as a powerful act of subversion. The inversion suggests a reversal of power, a reclaiming of the symbol of the cross from one of dominance and imposition to one of personal agency and resistance.

By hanging the crosses in this way, I am engaging with the narrative of St. Peter but recontextualizing it within the history of colonialism and forced conversion. The upside-down crosses call attention to the forced imposition of faith upon Indigenous and African populations in the Caribbean. They challenge the viewer to confront how Christianity was used as a tool of control and domination, and how the cross became a symbol of that oppressive power. But by presenting them inverted, I also propose a reversal of that narrative—a way to reclaim and reinterpret the cross on our own terms, much like St. Peter's act of choosing a different form of sacrifice.

The varying sizes of the crosses add another layer to the narrative, representing the diversity of experiences and the unequal weight of imposed faith across generations. Some crosses are small, almost delicate, while others are larger and more imposing, mirroring the spectrum of impact that Christianity had on colonized peoples. The diversity in size reflects how faith has been absorbed and experienced differently across communities, with some feeling its weight as a heavy burden, while others navigate it in subtler ways.

Suspending the crosses mid-air creates a sense of tension and disorientation. The viewer must navigate between them, encountering these symbols at different levels and perspectives. The inverted nature of the crosses disrupts the expectation of reverence, forcing the viewer to engage with the crosses in a way that feels unsettling and reflective. The installation compels viewers to move and look from different angles, reinforcing the idea that faith is not a static or one-dimensional experience; it is something that evolves, shifts, and must be continuously questioned and reinterpreted.

This inversion is an invitation for viewers to reconsider their relationship with faith and the legacy of Christianity in colonized spaces. Just as St. Peter chose to be crucified differently, the upside-down orientation of these crosses invites a rethinking and re-appropriation of a symbol that has long been tied to power and control. It is a gesture that suggests humility, like Peter's, but also one of resistance, asking viewers to challenge the narratives they have inherited and to see beyond the surface.

"Crucifixión de la Indigna" becomes a space where viewers are asked to confront their own beliefs, inherited traditions, and the ways in which they shape identity. The clear acrylic and inverted positioning of the crosses allow for a reexamination of faith as both an oppressive force and a site for reclaiming spiritual autonomy. This work is not about rejecting faith; rather, it is about reclaiming it, transforming the cross from a tool of submission into a symbol of empowerment.

The installation, through its play of light, transparency, and inversion, calls for reflection and resistance. It is a reminder that faith, while heavy and laden with historical trauma, can also be redefined, much like the choice made by St. Peter. "Crucifixión de la Indigna" asks viewers to move beyond passive acceptance, to see through the structures that have been imposed, and to find a path that reclaims and honors their own spiritual and cultural identities.

PRAYER FOR "CRUCIFIXIÓN DE LA INDIGNA"

Oh, spirits of those who came before,Guides of the ancestors, voices of the silenced,
We call upon you in this place of reflection,
Where crosses hang and truths are revealed.

Blessed be the ones who carried the weight,
Who felt the burden of belief pressed upon their souls.
For every wound and every scar,
We honor your strength, your resilience, your spirit.

Let these crosses, turned upside down,
Be symbols of humility, of reclamation, of truth.
May they remind us to seek beyond the surface,
To see through the structures imposed upon us.

Oh St. Peter, who chose a different path,
Guide us in our journey of transformation.
Help us to turn the weight we carry
Into a source of power, a light that cannot be dimmed.

As we walk among these crosses, clear as water,
May our eyes open to the clarity of our heritage,

The strength of our ancestors, the resilience of our faith.
Let us reclaim what was once taken, and honor what endures.

Spirit of reversal, spirit of resistance,
Turn our burdens into blessings, our pain into power.
May we walk the path of humility, truth, and liberation,
Guided by the clarity of our ancestors' light.

Amen.

GOSPEL OF "RELIQUIAS DE MIS ABUELOS: ECHOES OF ANCESTRAL DEVOTION"

In the quiet of our hearts, we hold the relics of the past,
The treasures of those who walked before us, whose footsteps guide our path.
In the shadows of history, we find the light of our ancestors,
A flame that has never dimmed, a truth that cannot be silenced.

Blessed are the hands that carried these relics,
That held the figures of saints, the beads of prayer, and the totems of hope.
For in these hands was the power to endure, to bless, and to heal,
To preserve the echoes of devotion passed down through time.

These reliquias, these sacred echoes, speak of those who whispered prayers in the night,
Who lit candles for the sick, who laid their hands upon the earth and called forth life.
They are the memories etched in statues, the protection found in symbols,

The strength carried in the smallest objects,
imbued with the spirit of survival.

Let us remember the saints of our ancestors,
San Lazaro, who carried the wounds of the body yet walked with strength.
The elephants that adorned the shelves, tokens of memory,
Symbols of family, fortune, and the connections that endure.

In these reliquias, we see the faces of our grandmothers and grandfathers,
The way they carried the faith, the culture, the spirit of the land.
Through every hardship, they found devotion in the everyday,
Blessing their homes, their children, their world with every gesture of care.

Blessed be the relics that hold the stories,
The ones passed from hand to hand, from heart to heart.
For in them lies the memory of our people, the faith that anchored them,
The light that will guide us as we walk our own paths.
We honor these echoes, these sacred traces of our lineage,
For they remind us that we are never alone.
The past walks with us, the prayers of our ancestors protect us,
And the spirit of devotion continues to live within our hands.

May we carry these echoes with grace,
May we remember the power in every relic, every memory.
In the presence of our ancestors, we find our strength, our story, our truth.

Amen.

RAÍCES Y RECUERDOS – A LIVING FAMILY ARCHIVE

In the heart of my exhibition is "Raíces y Recuerdos," a family tree wall that transcends traditional representations of ancestry. Rather than depicting branches or a genealogical map, this wall is composed of an array of frames of different sizes, each holding family photos and artifacts that capture the essence of my lineage. It serves as a living archive, inviting viewers to connect with the past in an intimate and immersive way.

The frames, which vary in size and style, create a patchwork of stories. Some hold photographs of my grandparents, parents, and extended family—captured moments of joy, resilience, and daily life that have shaped our history. Others contain symbols and objects representing ancestors for whom no photographs exist. These stand in for those whose images were lost to time, migration, or circumstance, yet whose presence is still felt. By including these symbolic placeholders, I honor the invisible threads that connect us to our past, even when physical records are absent.

At the center of the wall is a video installation that animates some of the photos of my ancestors, almost bringing them back to life. In the video, their faces move subtly, and their gestures become animated. Some ancestors blow kisses, while others smile warmly or wave hello. This animation creates the illusion that they are present in the room with us, bridging the gap between past and present. The effect is both haunting and comforting, reminding viewers that the spirits of our ancestors are not far away; they live on in our memories and in the traces they left behind.

The decision to animate these photos is an attempt to breathe life into the images, allowing viewers to engage with my ancestors as living beings rather than distant figures from the past. The animation transforms the space into an environment where the past feels alive, and where family members, even those long gone, continue to connect and interact. Their smiles, gestures, and playful kisses become a way of saying, "We are still here," reminding us that our roots are living entities that carry forward through us.

The frames themselves, arranged in a mosaic-like pattern, create a sense of movement and fluidity. They are not lined up in a strict order; instead, they flow across the wall, inviting viewers to move closer, to lean in, and to spend time with each piece. This arrangement emphasizes that memory is not linear or neatly categorized; it is dynamic, shifting, and ever-changing. By framing my ancestors and their symbols in this way, I hope to encourage viewers to reflect on their own family histories as living and evolving narratives.

The objects used to represent those ancestors without photos—such as heirlooms, religious symbols, and other mementos—speak to the cultural and spiritual legacy they carried. These artifacts are as much a part of my family history as any photograph. They hold the power to evoke memories and emotions, connecting the viewer to stories of resilience, survival, and strength that were passed down through generations. By placing these objects alongside the photos, I create a dialogue between the visible and the invisible, the known and the unknown.

The video at the center, with its animated faces, acts as a focal point that draws the viewer's gaze. It becomes a portal into another time, allowing the viewer to feel the presence of my ancestors in a visceral way. The smiles, waves, and kisses bring warmth and familiarity, transforming the wall into a space where the past feels like part of the present—a reminder that we are never truly separated from those who came before us. The video, while animated, remains gentle and subtle, blending seamlessly with the still frames around it, creating a sense of continuity and connection.

The wall is illuminated softly, casting shadows that give depth to each frame and artifact. The lighting enhances the sense of life within the installation, as the shadows shift and move subtly with the viewer's presence. It creates an environment where the past feels alive, as if the ancestors themselves are stepping forward from the shadows to greet those who stand before them. The play of light and shadow emphasizes the idea that memory is not static; it moves, evolves, and reveals itself in layers.

"Raíces y Recuerdos" serves as a tribute to the generations who paved the way for me, honoring their stories and preserving their legacy. It is a reminder that while some family histories are captured in photos, others are carried in objects, gestures, and memories that cannot be framed. By animating the faces of my ancestors, I create a space where viewers can experience the feeling of connection with their own roots, recognizing that the past is not distant—it is alive, present, and always intertwined with who we are.

This family tree wall invites viewers into a space where they can engage with the stories of my family as if they are meeting them in person. It offers a moment to pause, reflect, and feel the warmth of ancestral presence, even if only for a brief moment. In doing so, "Raíces y Recuerdos" becomes more than just an installation; it transforms into an act of communion, a bridge connecting past and present, and a celebration of the lives and memories that continue to shape us.

PRAYER TO SAN LÁZARO

Oh blessed San Lázaro, healer of wounds and protector of the afflicted,
We call upon your strength and compassion.
You who carried the pain of illness with grace,
And walked with the humble and the forgotten,
Be with us now in our time of need.

Holy guardian of the suffering,
You who bring comfort to the weary,
We ask for your healing touch upon our bodies and our spirits.
May your strength flow through us,
Lifting the burdens we carry, easing the pain we bear.

San Lázaro, patron of the sick and the outcast,
You who know the struggle of each day,
Guide us with your wisdom and your light.
Help us to endure with faith and courage,
And find peace in the midst of our trials.

As you walked the path of the wounded,
May we walk beside you in strength and hope.
May your blessings pour upon us,
Bringing renewal to our bodies and clarity to our minds.

In your name, San Lázaro, we seek solace and protection.
May your spirit of healing surround us,
May your love and grace uplift us,
And may your example of compassion inspire us always.

Amen.

SAN LÁZARO – THE GUARDIAN OF GENERATIONS

Among the cherished pieces in my collection of ancestral relics is the statue of San Lázaro that I acquired after my grandmother passed. This statue, with its weathered features and reverent expression, has been in my family for generations. It was originally given to my grandmother by her father—my great-grandfather—passed down as a symbol of protection and faith. For as long as I can remember, San Lázaro has been a figure of comfort, healing, and devotion—a guardian watching over our family through generations of trials and triumphs.

San Lázaro, known as the patron of the sick and protector of the poor, carries with him the spirit of resilience and compassion. In our family, his statue was not just a representation of faith; it was an integral part of our daily lives and rituals. As a child, I remember the sight of his altar in my grandmother's home—a place of both simplicity and reverence, where he stood surrounded by offerings, candles, and symbols that reflected the strength of our family's devotion.

When my grandmother passed, I inherited this sacred figure, along with the responsibility of maintaining his altar. I made the decision to incorporate pieces of my family's history into his space, honoring the generations that have come before me. Among these elements are coconut shells from my great-grandfather's tree in Puerto Rico. These shells, rough and textured, hold the memory of the land where my family's roots began. The act of including them in the altar is a way of bridging the spiritual presence of San Lázaro with the physical space of my great-grandfather's home—connecting faith, land, and lineage in a single, sacred space.

San Lázaro's altar is a space of reflection and prayer, where the past and present coexist. The coconut shells rest at the base of the statue, representing both nourishment and the roots of our ancestry. They are symbols of strength, resilience, and the enduring spirit of our family's connection to Puerto Rico. When I hold these shells, I feel the presence of my great-grandfather, who planted the tree and watched it grow, just as my family has planted roots and grown through generations.

One of the most meaningful aspects of San Lázaro's altar is the offering of pennies that he receives. This practice has been passed down through my family, and it is a tradition rooted in gratitude and devotion. Pennies, though simple and humble, carry significant meaning in our culture. They symbolize abundance and prosperity, even when resources are scarce. By placing pennies at the feet of San Lázaro, we are offering a token of what we have, trusting that even the smallest offerings will be received with grace and will bring blessings in return.

The pennies also represent the spirit of reciprocity—an exchange between the believer and the divine. In our family's tradition, when we offer pennies, we ask for San Lázaro's protection and guidance, particularly for those who are struggling with illness or hardship. We believe that by giving, even in the smallest measure, we open ourselves to receiving blessings and healing. The act of placing pennies is both a gesture of faith and a promise of connection, a reminder that San Lázaro's presence is not distant or inaccessible but is deeply intertwined with the everyday life and struggles of our family.

When I kneel before his altar, I am reminded of the generations who have come before me—my grandmother, my great-grandfather, and all the ancestors who placed their trust in San Lázaro's healing power. The pennies scattered at his feet, the coconut shells holding the memory of our homeland, and the light of the candles all come together to create a sacred space where faith, family, and memory are intertwined. It is a space where I feel the presence of my grandmother and great-grandfather, who, like me, turned to San Lázaro in times of need and gratitude.

The statue of San Lázaro, now in my care, is more than just an object of devotion; it is a living connection to my family's past, a reminder of the resilience and faith that have carried us through generations. By tending to his altar, by placing pennies and coconuts, I continue a tradition that honors my ancestors and keeps their spirits alive. This act of devotion is a way of acknowledging the healing power of faith and the unbreakable bonds that connect us to those who came before.

In the soft glow of the candles and the cool touch of the coconut shells, I feel the presence of San Lázaro and the strength of my family's faith. His statue, worn with time and full of memory, stands as a guardian over our home, a figure of hope and healing that will continue to watch over us for generations to come.

RECLAIMING FAITH – THE POWER OF RELIGIOUS SYMBOLISM"

Religious symbolism runs deep within my work, and for me, it is more than an aesthetic or cultural reference; it is a pathway to reclaim identity, reconnect with ancestry, and reshape our understanding of faith. Catholicism, with its rich iconography and rituals, was imposed upon my ancestors, often as a tool of control and oppression. Yet, over time, it has also become an integral part of how we connect to our past. For many of us, it is impossible to untangle our cultural identity from the religious practices that have been woven into our lineage, despite their colonial origins.

In my art and personal practice, I see the power of reclaiming and reframing these religious symbols. It is an act of resistance, a way to take back the tools that were once used to subjugate us and transform them into sources of strength and self-discovery. It is about claiming ownership over the narratives and symbols that have shaped us, choosing to exalt those elements of faith that speak to us, and rejecting those that do not. This process allows me, and others like me, to navigate the complex relationship between imposed religion and ancestral identity.

Catholicism was forced upon my ancestors as part of the colonization of the Caribbean, and for many generations, it served as a means of erasure—an attempt to replace the spiritual practices of the Taíno and African populations with the religion of the colonizers. But my ancestors, like so many others, adapted, integrated, and even transformed these imposed beliefs, creating hybrid practices that allowed them to retain their own spiritual heritage within the structure of Catholicism. This adaptation, seen in the syncretism between Catholic saints and African or Taíno deities, is a testament to the resilience and ingenuity of our people.

San Lázaro, for example, is not just a Catholic figure but also a syncretic symbol that merges elements of Catholic and African spiritual practices. For many in the Caribbean, San Lázaro is associated with Babalu Aye, an orisha of healing and illness in the Yoruba religion. By integrating these spiritual figures, our ancestors created a bridge between their traditional beliefs and the new religion imposed upon them. This merging of faiths allowed them to continue their spiritual practices under the guise of Catholicism, preserving their cultural identity even as they adapted to the realities of colonization.

This integration of Catholic symbolism is foundational to our culture, and it is essential that we honor and reclaim it in our own way. For me, this means using the symbols, saints, and rituals that have been passed down to reframe my connection to faith and ancestry. It is about reclaiming Catholicism—not as a symbol of colonial dominance, but as a space where my ancestors left traces of themselves, transforming what was once used to erase them into a language of resilience and survival.

My work seeks to honor this transformation by using Catholic symbols—crosses, saints, and altars—not as they were originally intended by the colonizers but as sites of personal and cultural reclamation. In doing so, I create a space where viewers can engage with these symbols, not as imposed structures but as chosen ones. I reframe the meaning of these objects, allowing them to become sources of empowerment, memory, and connection to ancestry.

For example, when I place crosses in my installations, I am not using them to represent suffering or submission, but to reclaim the power of choice. I exalt those who carried the weight of faith on their own terms, transforming the cross from a symbol of oppression into one of resilience. When I incorporate saints like San Lázaro, I am not simply honoring the Catholic saint; I am also invoking the orisha behind him, the spiritual strength that my ancestors carried in their hearts despite the demands of conversion.

Reframing these symbols also involves the freedom to choose who or what we exalt. We are no longer bound to the narratives imposed upon us; we have the agency to decide which figures hold meaning for us. This freedom allows us to create our own spiritual paths, shaped by the intersections of our cultural and ancestral identities. In my work, this might look like honoring my grandmothers alongside the saints, creating altars that blend the traditional with the personal, or elevating figures from Taíno history and African spirituality alongside the icons of Catholicism.

This act of reframing is essential in understanding our identity and forming our own paths. It allows us to engage with the complexity of our heritage, acknowledging the painful history of forced conversion while also celebrating the strength and adaptability of our ancestors who took the tools given to them and made them their own. It is a recognition that while Catholicism was a colonial imposition, it has also become a foundational part of our culture—one that we have the right to transform and redefine.

In reclaiming these symbols, we are not rejecting the influence of Catholicism; we are reshaping it. We are choosing to see beyond the narrative of conquest and finding the ways in which our ancestors wove their own stories into the fabric of the faith they were forced to adopt. We are honoring the ways in which they resisted erasure, creating new traditions, and preserving their spiritual practices within a faith that was used against them.

For me, this process is not just about reclaiming symbols; it is about reclaiming power. It is about deciding for myself who and what is sacred, and it is about creating a space where others can do the same. We have the freedom to exalt our ancestors, our struggles, our resilience, and our spiritual connections—whether they come from the Catholic saints or the Taíno deities, the orishas or the spirits of the land. It is a freedom to redefine faith on our terms, to create new paths that honor where we come from while allowing us to shape where we are going.

In the end, the act of reclaiming religious symbolism is about honoring our history, recognizing the ways our ancestors adapted, and choosing to carry forward the elements of faith that empower us. It is a process of turning a symbol of oppression into a source of pride, and a means of transforming imposed structures into spaces where our voices, stories, and identities can thrive. It is a way of saying that despite the past, despite the imposition, we are the ones who get to decide how we move forward, and we do so carrying the strength, faith, and spirit of all those who came before us.

SPELL TO CLOSE THE DOORS OF SPIRIT

MATERIALS NEEDED:

- A small bowl of salt (for protection)
- A white candle (for closure and peace)
- A sprig of rosemary or sage (for cleansing)

INSTRUCTIONS:

Prepare the Space:
Find a quiet place where you can sit undisturbed. Light the white candle and hold the sprig of rosemary or sage in your hand. Take a deep breath, feeling the energy around you begin to settle.

Circle of Salt:
Sprinkle a small circle of salt around your space. As you do this, say:

> "Salt of earth, create a seal,
> Close the doors, protect, and heal."

Cleansing the Space:
Wave the sprig of rosemary or sage through the flame of the candle and then pass it around your space. As you cleanse, say:

> "By this herb and light so bright,

I seal the doors, I end the night.
Spirits called, return to rest,
With peace and grace, I close this quest."

Final Prayer:
Place your hand over your heart and take a deep breath, feeling calm and grounded. Speak this prayer:

"Spirits kind, I thank you now,
For hearing my call, for showing me how.
I close the doors, I end the spell,
Return in peace, all is well.
As I will, so it shall be,
With love, with light, I set you free."

Extinguish the Candle:
Blow out the candle, feeling the space clear and peaceful. Brush away the salt, knowing the doors are now closed.

The spell is complete. Carry the sense of peace with you as you move forward, knowing all energies have returned to rest.

CLOSING HYMN: IN THE ECHOES OF ANCESTRY

In the echoes of the past, we find our way,
Through whispered prayers and light of day.
The paths we walk, the stories told,
Guide us back to roots of old.

Blessed be the hands that paved our road,
With strength and love, our lives bestowed.
For every struggle, every song,
They carried us through, made us strong.

Oh ancestors, we honor you now,
With hearts wide open, we humbly bow.
The faith you held, the dreams you spun,
Live on in us, as days are done.

In the light of the moon, in the rise of the sun,
We walk the path you've always begun.
With grace and courage, we seek our own,
Yet your strength remains, the seeds you've sown.

Blessed be the earth, the sky, the sea,
The land that holds our memory.
And may we find, in every breath,
The love that outlasts even death.

As we close this book, may we carry forth,
The stories of our past, our sacred worth.
In the echoes of the ancestors' song,
May we find the place where we belong.

Amen.

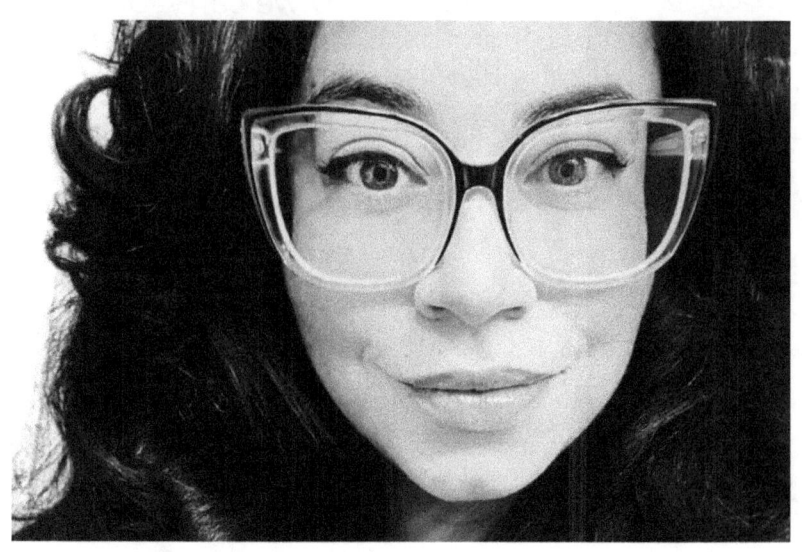

About the Author

Denise "The Vamp DeVille" Zubizarreta (b. 1984) is a neurodivergent mixed media interdisciplinary artist and cultural operations specialist of Puerto Rican and Cuban descent, with over a decade of experience in various creative fields. She is currently an arts and culture writer for Hyperallergic, Southwest Contemporary, Latina Media Co., Daria, Variable West, and Artfully Employed that offer curated and critical perspectives on contemporary arts and culture.

Denise holds a B.F.A. in Fine Art from the Rocky Mountain College of Art + Design (RMCAD), and is completing her Masters in Arts Leadership and Cultural Management (M.A.L.C.M.) at Colorado State University. Her passion for arts and culture drives her to explore and challenge the intersections of post-colonial theory, identity, technology and traditions in her writing and mixed media works.